Also by Lois Wyse

NONFICTION
Company Manners
The Six-Figure Woman
Lovetalk
Mrs. Success
Funny, You Don't Look Like a Grandmother
Kid, You Sing My Songs

FICTION
The Granddaughter
Far from Innocence
Kiss, Inc.
The Rosemary Touch
Seconds

POETRY
Love Poems for the Very Married
Are You Sure You Love Me?
A Weeping Eye Can Never See
Love Poems for a Rainy Day

Grandchildren are so much fun, I should have had them first

Lois Wyse

Illustrated by Lilla Rogers

Random House Large Print

THIS LARGE PRINT BOOK CARRIES
THE SEAL OF APPROVAL OF N.A.V.H.

Copyright © 1992 by Garret Press, Inc.
Illustrations © 1992 by Lilla Rogers

Published by Crown Publishers, Inc., 201 East 50th Street, New York, New York 10022. Member of the Crown Publishing Group.

CROWN is a trademark of Crown Publishers, Inc.
Manufactured in the United States of America

Library of Congress Cataloging-in-Publication Data

Wyse, Lois.
    Grandchildren are so much fun, I should have had them first / by Lois Wyse.
        p.   cm.

    1. Grandparents—Humor.   2. Grandparent and child—Humor.
I. Title.
PN6231.G8W97   1992b
814′.54—dc20   92-50240
                                                        CIP

ISBN 0-517-59297-5
10 9 8 7 6 5 4 3 2 1
First Edition

For the family
of grandchildren
we love with
all our hearts

CONTENTS

LOOK WHO'S A GRANDPARENT

"WHO'S THAT LADY ON THE TREADMILL?" "THAT'S NO LADY. THAT'S MY GRANDMA."

OVER THE HILLS AND THROUGH THE WOODS TO GRANDMOTHER'S CONDO WE GO

GRANDFATHERS ARE TO LOVE

Look
who's
a
Grandparent
!

I CAN'T BELIEVE IT'S ME

Just when you thought it was safe to walk past the baby store and go directly to the travel agent, you get the news that puts your life on hold.

A baby?

Your babies are having babies?

Of course you're thrilled to be a grandparent—sort of.

But let's face it. Didn't it happen just a wee bit early?

Of course this is wonderful news.

But now?

Who said you wanted it now?

But it doesn't matter what you want or when you want it because grandmotherhood is the only state in life a woman reaches without first saying yes, and grandfatherhood is the only state a man reaches without first voicing an opinion.

In fact, if asked their opinions about becoming grannies, a lot of men and women would say, "No, thanks, not just yet," for we live in a world where short-skirted grandmas boogie to the beat of life and golf-playing grandpas dream of shooting their age.

We are the generation that came of age in an ageless society.

Nobody looks like a grandmother.

Nobody feels like a grandfather.

But, ready or not, here come our grandchildren!

In Stamford, a thirty-eight-year-old woman, when told she was going to be a grandmother, proved that she wasn't ready for lavender and lace by announcing her own pregnancy and delivering her baby a few weeks after her grandchild was born.

On the other hand, a thirty-eight-year-old woman in Detroit was so distressed at the prospect of becoming a thirty-something grandmother that she refused to discuss baby-naming, didn't attend one baby shower, and never shopped for a layette. But, when Baby was born, New Granny went to the hospital, took one look at her infant grandson, burst into tears of joy, and hasn't been able to spend a day away from the boy ever since.

That was seven years ago.

A San Diego grandmother who skis the grown-up slopes was given a shocking pink ski jacket for Christmas. When poured into her ski pants and zipped into her jacket, she didn't look like anybody's Grandma. She looked more like one of the snow bunnies.

So, as she went off to ski The Big One with her family, she suggested that her children and grandchildren stop referring to her as a grandmother. Even the word *mother* seemed a bit much. So the kids agreed that they would yell and spell up and down the slopes, "M-O-M."

And so they did.

"M-O-M, over here the snow is great," a son would call. And off went the pink flash.

"Meet me on Number Seven, M-O-M," shouted one daughter with her daughter in tow. And off went dear old M-O-M.

Finally a handsome young man turned on his skis to one of M-O-M's kids. "M-O-M?" he inquired hesitantly. "Does that mean she's your mom?"

"Yes," was the answer.

He stood openmouthed as the pink jacket flashed by. Then he grinned. "You guys sure got yourself one hot mama."

Ever since that day M-O-M has insisted on being called Mom and Grandma and watching the faces when people learn that the cute kid in the pink outfit is not only one hot mama, she is one hot grandmama.

And that's the real news on the granny front.

Grandmothers aren't hot from cooking and baking these days.

Grandmoms are hot because they're swimming in the mainstream of life.

Modern-day grandfathers aren't into pipes and slippers. They're more likely to own guitars and running shoes.

See?

There really is life after grandparenting.

So here's to life.

Here's to grandparents.

And here's to life with grandparents.

Long may it last!

WHICH ONE IS THE GRANDMOTHER?

ou know why you can't tell which one is the grandmother?

Because the mother, frazzled and frangible, looks a bit older than she is. That's what walking the floor at night, settling more arguments than a U.N. negotiator, and never wearing lipstick does to you.

The grandmother, on the other hand, looks much younger than she is. That's because she is the one who is renewed, reanimated, and removed from the dailiness of child rearing. In her cute clothes and with her perky haircut and perfect makeup, she looks almost girlish.

But should they be women you don't know, you'll soon be able to tell which one is the grandmother because

When
a child hits a sibling and says, "You idiot . . ."
The Mother Is the One Who
separates the children instantly while visions of Cain and Abel dance in her head.
The Grandmother Is the One Who
shrugs and walks away mumbling, "So what else is new?"

15

When

a child cries for a cookie,

The Mother Is the One Who

puts her foot down and says sternly, "No. You have already had enough sweets today. You are allowed a nutritional snack instead. Here's a peach."

The Grandmother Is the One Who

puts an arm around the child and murmurs, "Don't cry. Here are two cookies because I love you so much."

When

a three-year-old is still awake at 11 P.M.,

The Mother Is the One Who

walks the floor, gets the water, brings the cracker, reads the story, and wonders what she did to deserve a child who won't go to bed.

The Grandmother Is the One Who

looks on in amazement and remembers gratefully that Dr. Spock never would have permitted such nonsense.

NEW KIDS ON THE BLOCK

hey never call after 10 P.M. It's not a family rule, but rather one of those things that children do or don't do. In our case they don't phone after 10 P.M.

So, when the call came at 10:30 or so, I was anxious as I heard my husband say, "Hi, Denise, how's everything?" What was happening with Rob and her? Who had fallen out of a tree? Why was anybody in a tree at night anyway? Who— oh, you know the dark side of imagination.

But Bud sounded at ease as he handed me the phone.

"Hi," Denise said softly, almost shyly.

"Yes?" I had that anxious mother edge to my voice.

"Mom . . ." There was a pause. "I'm pregnant."

"Pregnant?" I don't know which was greater, my relief or my surprise. Only weeks earlier Denise and I had talked about her return to the work world now that both her children were going to school.

"I guess I won't need any job advice," she laughed.

And, with that call, my family of eight grand-children grew to nine.

The funny part is that Bud, a widower who was my equal at eight when he married widowed me, was informed of the anticipated birth of his ninth grandchild only weeks before Denise was due.

And so it came to be that on our first wedding anniversary, unlike most newlyweds, we had two new babies.

Eighteen grandchildren, and no two alike.

Some are similar, of course.

There are ways that Josie resembles Molly—both mothers see that.

But Josie and Molly are cousins only by marriage—our marriage. Still, they are more alike than Molly and her natural cousin Stephanie or Josie and her sister Lindsay.

Ah, there's nothing like heredity.

FAX ME NO QUESTIONS

Liz is the first in the neighborhood, the first to be notified of grandmotherhood by fax.

"I was horrified," she admits. "Imagine getting a fax saying, 'Dear Granny, Emma Sue has arrived.' No size. No weight. No news of the new mother, my daughter. I am an old-fashioned grandmother accustomed to the hurried call from the pay station just off the delivery room, the call from the father that tells me all is fine, how long the labor was, how long the baby is, how long before I can see New Mommy and child. Of course, in all fairness to the new parents I'll admit that I was in Oregon with a client, and they were in Vermont, and no one knew quite how to reach me, but still there are limits to what we grannies accept, and I was dying for details. This family had just moved to a little town in Vermont, so I didn't even know the name of the hospital where my daughter and new granddaughter were. There would be no one at their house, of course, so how could I get information? I called my middle daughter, the lawyer who lives in New York."

"Oh, Mother," she said in her old teenage voice when she realized that it was only her mom on the phone. "I'm very busy now."

"But have you heard the news about your sister?"

"Which sister?" she asked impatiently.

"Your older sister, the new mother; that's who."

"Oh. Her. Yes, I heard, but I really can't talk. I'm filing a brief."

"Then just tell me the name of the hospital where I can reach her."

There was a long pause. "I don't know."

"You don't know?" Liz's voice went up in shock and disbelief.

"Well, it's somewhere in Vermont."

"Yes, but which hospital? What's the name?"

"There's only one hospital in their town," middle daughter volunteered, "so maybe they're there. Now really, Mother, I'm so busy. I can't talk—"

"I didn't call to talk to you," her mother reminded her, not without a hint of exasperation and annoyance. "I want to talk to your sister."

"Call their town and ask information for the name of the only hospital," the lawyer/daughter responded with a sensible display of lawyerlike skills.

So Liz called information and found a pleasant-voiced woman on the other end of the line. It was the kind of voice you could tell your troubles to. "Please give me the name and number of the only hospital in town," Liz said, realizing that her voice probably had an urgent edge.

Without a moment's hesitation she was given the hospital name and number.

Liz dialed, and as she heard the call go through, she felt relief. In just a few minutes she'd be talking to the new mother. But wait. Which name had New Mommy used? Her married name? Her maiden name, which was her professional name? Liz made an executive decision. She asked for her daughter by both names.

There was a pause. "We have no one by either of those names," she heard. Now the voice did not sound so friendly.

"You must," Liz insisted. "It's my daughter, and she is in maternity."

"Maternity?"

"Yes, she's a new mother. She's my daughter—"

"Excuse me," the receptionist interrupted, "but are you sure she's here? You see, this is a retirement home."

Eventually Liz connected with the new mother and child, and now all is well.

But Liz has told her daughters, "Let's get something straight. From now on when your mother tells you she wants the facts, she doesn't mean the fax."

THE ADOPTABLE GRANNY

Lorrie had a dollhouse, dolls, and a teeny-weeny pram.

All that was in the kindergarten of her life, and as she grew older and discarded her toys for the real world, she waited for the day when she would replace her toy baby parapher-nalia with the real things—beginning, of course, with her own child.

Still, six years after her marriage there was no baby.

Lorrie tried all the new chemistry of pregnancy. Nothing worked.

Finally her husband, Steve, said, "Let's face it, sweetie. It's adopt or nothing for us."

"Adopt," she said quickly.

Adoption, however, is one of those life events that's easier desired than accomplished. It took two more years of waiting before Steve and Lorrie had a phone call informing them that there would be a baby for them, a baby to be born in five months.

Lorrie could hardly wait to call her mother. At last her mother could be just like all the other mothers with the gold credit cards and the big smiles and the excited sense of planning a new generation to love.

"We're getting a baby," Lorrie shouted excitedly.

"Oh," was the cool, distant response.

"A baby of our own," Lorrie said triumphantly.

"Well, not of *our* own," her mother added.

"Mother!" Lorrie's voice was filled with shock and dismay. Her mother knew how she'd longed for a child, how hard it had been for her and Steve, and to have this life goal greeted with this—this indifference. It was too much. "Mother, this is *our* baby."

"*Yours*," her mother replied, "not *ours*."

Lorrie sat quietly by the phone for many minutes after her conversation with her mother. Then she decided to call her father. Surely he would feel differently. Hadn't Lorrie always been Daddy's girl?

But her father was even colder than her mother. "I don't believe in adoption," he said in his matter-of-fact lawyer voice. "Who knows what you're taking into your home? It's bad enough if problems are born to you. Why go out and adopt them?"

So this is the way it would be. Their baby would be loved and wanted by its parents and rejected by its only grandparents. Steve's parents had died years ago.

How unfair, Lorrie thought. And how cruel, too. How could her parents hurt her and this unborn child so deeply?

Lorrie knew that she needed to talk to someone, someone older, someone who would understand, and so she called her neighbor Martha. Martha had been the buyer in a large department store, and when her store had been merged and submerged, Martha had parachuted out at just about the time she'd have retired.

Martha gave Lorrie both tea and sympathy, patted her hand, smiled, and said, "Well, this doesn't have to be such a sad story, Lorrie. I think your baby should have a grandmother, so why don't you adopt me?"

Lorrie's eyes widened. "You?"

"Why not?" Martha shrugged. "I know all about grandmothering. My own daughter couldn't have children, went ahead and adopted two. I'm their grandmother—and who ever said a bloodline was a heartline? Don't worry about another thing. I'm right here in the neighborhood, and I can sit for you and help in a hundred ways."

"You'll do all that for us?" Lorrie asked in amazement.

"Of course I will. But I'm not waiting five months for that child."

"What do you mean?" Lorrie asked.

"I can help you more than any other grandmother right now. You see, we'll have to buy a layette, and I still get my store discount. Who deserves it more than my newest grandchild?"

THE MAKING OF A GRANDMOTHER

ybil is extraordinary by anyone's standards. She had 800s on her SATs, is pretty, plays two instruments, and has a lot of friends.

It was no surprise that she chose to follow in the footsteps of several male family members who are doctors. And it was no surprise that she was consistently at the top of her class, was admitted to a fine medical school, and had no trouble getting internships and residencies.

Her field is pediatrics, and because she'd always loved children, her parents knew that one day she'd want a child of her own.

It was only after she went into practice that they realized that Sybil would probably never have children, for she came home one day and told them that she and her lover were making plans to live together, to have a life together. Her lover was a nurse, a woman she'd met at the hospital.

"If this is what you want," her parents said— and they said it not with rancor or anger but with satisfied acceptance, for they truly did believe that Sybil was entitled to live her life in any way she wanted.

Last year Sybil told her parents that she was about to make a lifetime dream come true.

She and her lover were planning to have a child.

They had decided that through *in vitro* fertilization Sybil would be the biological mother, and both lovers would share the parenting of the child.

When Sybil became pregnant, her mother called her lover's mother, and the two grandmothers-to-be went with the couple to buy the baby's layette, outfit the nursery.

The healthy baby was born just a year ago.

"It's not the way I thought things would be," Sybil's mother admits, "but my daughter is happy, and I'm here to make sure that this new baby has two sets of grandparents who get along just fine and who are there with love and emotional support. What we grandparents have to remember is that the future doesn't belong to us, and we'd better not get so attached to the past that we lose our kids along the way. I know that Sybil always wanted to be a mother, and I'm thankful that she is."

My Grandchild, the next Albert Einstein

WHEN I GROW UP . . .

Nobody grows up hoping to be a grandmother.

Mother? Yes.

Grandmother? No way.

What little girl at play turns to her best friend and insists, "I'll be the grandmother. You be the baby."

No, what they say is, "I'll be the mother. You be the baby."

Who wouldn't want to be the mother?

She's the one with responsibility and authority, the next best thing to princess.

Why would any little girl dream of being a grandmother?

Who wants to sit alone in the backseat while the parents talk to one another up front?

Who wants to groan as her old bones protest when she stands up and moan whenever she reverses positions and sits?

Who's anxious to advance the clock and pretend she has white hair and wrinkles?

Who aspires to longer skirts and shorter breath?

Who?

Parents, that's who.

Daughter Kathy called after a day of Molly-coddling during the year her child Molly was putting her through the Reign of Terror by Twos.

"You're so lucky," Kathy moaned. "You never need a sitter. You don't have to stay here and listen to the ravings of a two-year-old. You can go out whenever you want and talk to grown-ups, and the child who's screaming in the super-market is never yours. Oh, what I wouldn't give just to be the grandmother for about five years. And then let's see how Molly will handle her child."

Marlene agrees. Marlene is the woman who readily admits, "I'm *plotzing* to be a grandmother. Of course, my children are only nine and twelve, but I figure that anything is better than this."

THE OLD PROS

eth is nothing if not a pragmatist. She's the grandmother who bought the babies cribs, blankets, and bonds. The other grandmother supplied the lace dresses, cunning velvet suits, and Steiff animals.

Therefore, when her fifth grandchild was a few months old, Beth was taken aback by a phone call from her daughter-in-law, Nancy.

"Beth," she said in her breathy little voice (Nancy belongs to the I Call My Mother-in-Law by Her First Name School), "can you be at our apartment tomorrow morning at ten-thirty?"

"What's the problem?"

"No problem. This is just for your fun. Tomorrow the baby's doing fruit."

"Doing fruit? Are you trying to say that the kid's eating peaches?"

"Yes, and I knew you'd want to watch."

Beth scratched her head. Doesn't this child know I'm a five-timer? Doesn't she know I don't need another dress ruined by a kid eating first peaches? So Beth said what all mothers and mothers-in-law say when asked to join the family for an epic event, "Of course I'll be there. What time does the show end?"

"You ought to be out by noon if all goes well."

Beth shook her head disbelievingly and called Helene.

"Helene, you know we're supposed to meet at noon tomorrow? Well, make it twelve-thirty."

"Any problem?"

"No problem. It's just that the new baby's doing peaches."

Helene laughed. "What are you supposed to do? Videotape it for the future generations?"

"No, the proud father will do that. I just have to be there. I'm the audience."

"Oh well, remember that it gets better. You know, I just had my eighth grandchild and when my daughter and her husband took the two older children on a vacation weekend, I offered to baby-sit. Frankly, I wanted to bond with a new three-month-old I've not even looked at. Every time I go over there I'm afraid I'm going to offend the Alreadys."

"The Alreadys?"

"You know. The grandchildren who were already here when the new one came. So when I stayed with the baby, I cooked and I cuddled, and

I explained that I am the grandmother she should really love because look how terrific I am even now when she does nothing but perform the most elementary human functions. But you know something, Beth? All new babies are just like peaches. Once you've seen peaches—let's face it, it's not Paris—once you've seen peaches, and once you've changed a diaper, you don't need to prove you're really a grandmother by doing it again and again."

"You're right," Beth admitted, "but if you think I'm going to tell that to my daughter-in-law, then you don't understand why I'm telling you to meet me a half hour later."

GOING, GOING, GONE

hey're not yet grandparents, but they are two stops past Kids 'R' Us, so the license plate on their hot little two-seat sports car reads, "KDSRGON."

Confessions of a Grandfather: "Grandparenting is not at all what I expected. I actually look forward to taking my grandson to a ball game. Strange. You see, my kids were never my pals, but my grandchildren are."

Charlene confesses that she is not the ever-available grandmother. "I'm not at all what I expected to be," she admits. "Here I am, over fifty and alone. You'd think I'd want that baby all the time, but I don't. Oh, it's not that I avoid him, but I find I want him on my own turf at my own times. I call my daughter-in-law and say, 'I'll take Patrick this weekend.' How strange it is. Although I'm alone, in some ways I'm busier than my daughter-in-law. I don't think she always understands, and I don't know that my son even notices. It's just that for the first time life is about me, and I like it much more than the world wanted me to think I would."

NEATNESS COUNTS

When Mac and Rosemary's son Kerry married Blythe, everyone waited to see what kind of housekeeper Blythe would be. The world knew that she was a lawyer with courtroom competence; now the world waited to see how she performed around the house because Blythe had married into a family where neatness counts.

"Our house is so antiseptic you could perform a heart transplant in the living room," Mac used to say. But he said it uncomplainingly. Indeed those words seemed to be uttered with both affection and pride.

But after only a few weeks of marriage Mac and Rosemary knew the sad truth. Their son had married a slob. The only one who seemed not to notice was Kerry, the new husband. "After all these years with us, he must see the dirt around him," Rosemary moaned to Mac. Mac shrugged. "I don't understand it at all," he admitted.

But both Rosemary and Mac held their tongues, and they were rewarded when, after three years of marriage, Blythe and Kerry named their firstborn Rosemary after her grandmother.

Once the initial glow of grandmotherhood faded, the new grandparents found more mess than ever overflowing in the professional family's apartment. "It breaks my heart," Grandmother Rosemary would say to Mac, "to visit and see muffin crumbs on the sofa, handprints on the walls. Still, Baby Rosemary is a dear little girl, and she seems none the worse for being raised in an upscale slum."

One day as Grandmother Rosemary was visiting, the baby dropped a glass of juice. Granny rushed to mop, but Mama Blythe stopped her. "Why mop it up? She'll only spill it again."

Grandmother Rosemary demurred modestly. She had no desire to argue with a lawyer, especially a lawyer daughter-in-law. Kerry, who witnessed the whole scene, stood by and said nothing. "Can you believe this, Mac?" Rosemary asked her husband that evening. "Kerry stood there and said not one word, even after I explained to him later—a lot later, after Blythe had left the room—that I was only doing this for his family."

As time went by, Kerry and Baby Rosemary continued to live in what Grandma could only call "Blythe's mess." Grandmother's remarks became more pointed, but they seemed to have no influence on Kerry.

"I'm at wits' end," Rosemary admitted to Mac.

It was just about that time that Blythe and Kerry asked Rosemary and Mac to baby-sit from time to time.

Grandmother Rosemary smiled. She knew

she was about to win the war over dirt.

Each time she was asked to sit, Grandmother Rosemary eagerly accepted with the understanding that Baby Rosemary be brought to their home and put in the nursery she and Mac set up.

When Baby Rosemary took to flinging her muffin from her crib, Granny did not chastise the child. Instead she showed Baby Rosemary how to clean up after herself. Pretty soon the muffin throwing stopped because once she understood the rules, Baby Rosemary decided that it took less effort to follow them than to disobey them. But finally the day came when Little Rosemary, now five, started to ask some serious questions.

"Nana," she said to her grandmother one day, "why is your house so clean?"

Rosemary paused. "Do you like it this way?"

"Yes," her granddaughter answered. "But why do you do it? Why do you go around with a rag cleaning up after us? Why don't you go to work and just forget about the dirt?"

She looked at her granddaughter. "Because clean is my work," she explained. "Your mommy goes to the office and does her work. My work is here at home, and my job is to keep us all clean."

"My mommy says this is control," the five-year-old announced solemnly.

"What did you hear about control?" There was an icy fear in Rosemary's voice.

"Huh?" Little Rosemary asked.

"What does 'control' mean?" the nervous grandmother asked.

"Well, I'm not sure," the little girl confessed. "All I know is that Mommy says we all love you, and isn't it too bad you keep trying to make us all as clean as you. My mommy says it's all about control, and it's just your way of holding on to Daddy."

Just then Little Rosemary looked out the window. "Nana, it's a butterfly on the bush," she shouted animatedly as she ran outside, banging the screen door behind her.

But Rosemary didn't even hear the screen door bang. The echo of the child's words was too loud in her head.

And that night, for the first time in memory, Rosemary did not plump the living room cushions and empty the dishwasher before she went to bed.

But to Rosemary the strangest part was that Mac didn't even seem to notice.

VIVA LA DIFFERENCE

t was very different this time.

No question about this new baby.

It was already a she, confirmed by science.

And Stephanie, the seven-year-old sister, had already confided that the new granddaughter was to be named Emily.

So there would be no surprises this time.

And now, the day after the birth, I was flying—flying as I had each time before—to see a new granddaughter.

The old anxiety over what grandmothering will be like was replaced by the new relaxed questions:

Will the baby look like the mother's or the father's family?

Will she be a crier?

Will Stephanie and Alex, the children in the family, be excited about Baby Emily after she's two weeks old or will she be like a toy they tire of? What will tuitions be in the twenty-first century?

Just the ordinary everyday grandmotherly concerns of the 1990s.

Still, as the miles rolled by, so did the memories.

I relived the births of other grandchildren, the hospital-masked and -gowned parents, the look-but-don't-touch days after birth, and I landed feeling slightly nostalgic and a bit removed from the reality of the moment.

And so I went to the hospital, fully anticipating a rerun of the births of Baby Emily's siblings.

But the hospital had changed since Stephanie was born.

Now there was a sunny atrium where there used to be a dismal entryway.

And when I went up to the maternity floor, no one questioned me. That's when I found that grandparents, parents, and siblings can visit whenever they want.

Visit whenever they want?

But what about the other babies in the nursery?

I looked in the nursery.

There were no other babies.

I should not have been that surprised because only a week before we'd had a new baby on Bud's side of the family—his son Joe and Jennifer also had a new daughter. And not only had Bud been at the hospital for her birth, he'd been in the delivery room.

And when we went to visit Baby Lyn she was in her mommy's room.

Still, I thought that may have been a courtesy peculiar to that hospital and that city.

But now I went to Denise's room, and there was a tiny crib holding this tiny new baby. No wonder there were no other babies in the nursery. They were all rooming with their mothers.

But even had I had to pick out this baby in a nursery, I'd have known this was Emily, for here was no ordinary red-faced squalling child.

Emily was small and beautiful and—and she looked exactly as Rob had looked the day he was born. Rob with his head of dark hair and big eyes and dimpled chin. Here was my son now appearing as a perfectly formed little girl.

My eyes could not hold the tears of joy and thanksgiving.

The mother and baby had both come through. All was well.

And we had a new baby who belonged to all of us.

"Hold her. It's all right," my son assured me.

Then, miracle of miracles, as I picked her up

and held her close, she picked up her head and looked at me.

I know that I'm supposed to believe that new-born babies can't really pick up their heads and see—Emily was now nineteen hours old—but no one could ever convince me, for I was holding a new life, a fresh chance, another promise that although lives we love end, lives we will love begin.

There were supposed to be no grandmother surprises this time, I reminded myself.

And yet there was surprise.

Surprise that still my heart could turn, my eyes could fill, and toward this small, unknowing child, I could know such feeling.

How could I have forgotten that each time, each birth is not only a first for the baby but a renewal for all of us who will love and cherish her?

How could I have failed to realize that for us grandparents the only difference is number?

The love is always the same.

Before Lyn was born, Jennifer asked whether we'd feel differently because this wasn't the first grandchild for Bud or for me.

We'd quickly assured her that there would be

no difference.

Still, there is nothing like a new baby in one's arms to reinforce the old commitments of love and care.

WHAT'S MY LINE?

e, four grandmothers and I, met in the Green Room at a television show. We certainly weren't as interesting as those people you see on Phil and Oprah and Geraldo; not one of us had a "it shouldn't happen to you" life story. Indeed we all had rather nice stories. Not a whole lot of crabgrass in our gardens.

Now we were facing the cameras and the world, newsworthy not just because we were grandmothers but because we were women with careers at the grandmother stage of life.

One of our group, age sixty-four, was a stand-up comic. At sixty-two she had switched from teaching at a college to joke-telling at a comedy club.

Why did she wait until sixty-two? someone asked.

"Wait?" she asked wide-eyed. "I didn't wait.

This is early. You know sixty-two to ninety-two are the funny years."

Well, maybe they are. Perhaps we concentrate too much on how far we used to throw the ball, how fast we once ran the mile, and the ways we dined and danced the night away. Maybe the real humor is that we never did do any of it all that well. Maybe it's true that we have kind of fumbled and stumbled our way to this place, and maybe it is time for a last good laugh. Perhaps it is only memory that dances gracefully over the years, not people, and it's time we saw the humor in our vain pretensions.

The grannies with me that day, however, were not growing old with memories. Instead they were staying young with action. One of the grandmas was a motorcycle rider, one an airplane test pilot, and the fourth was a model for Jockey underwear.

Each admitted that on occasion she meets with a raised eyebrow, a few "ahems," and an incredulous "I can't believe that's what you do for a living" look. But these grandmothers take it all in stride because one universal among career grandmas is that each learns to develop a tough hide. She doesn't fall apart at the first sound of

criticism, the first indication of someone asking, "But how could you even consider that at your age?"

They're resolute, a little scared, but pleased to be a little different from everybody else. Somehow I sense that this is the way they were when they raised their families.

That sense of derring-do is developed early but refined later. The woman who stands up in a town meeting to express her views is tomorrow's sky diver. Nowadays the early years serve as preparation for the important actions we'll be brave enough and strong enough to perform.

Who knows which of today's moms will be the pioneer in the laboratory? Who among us will fly off to the nearest planet or zip around her factory on her motorcycle?

Age is not a barrier; it is a support. Wise decisions are made by people of experience.

So look out, world!

Ready or not, here comes a whole generation of grannies in black lace and black leather.

But as we all go speeding off into the sunset filling new roles, it does make one wonder who will fill old cookie jars.

GENERATIONS OF LOVE

orky talked to her grandson Charles by telephone almost every day, and just before she hung up, Corky always said, "Don't forget Grandma loves you."

Charles was six years old before he realized that Corky's full name was not Grandma Loves You.

Because they all married young and produced progeny without delay, their family has five living generations. So the brand-new grandmother decided to have a picture taken of the group.

Wearing their best outfits, they all lined up: the new grandmother, her daughter, her daughter's daughter, her mother, and her grandmother. Five generations of women.

The new grandmother cuddled the new grandchild, who responded with soft coos. "See?" chortled New Grandmother to her grandmother. "She loves me."

Great-great-grandmother smiled. "She knows her granny."

"No, no," insisted New Grandmother. "She

won't call me Granny. She will call me Gammy."

"Hmmmmmpf," snorted Great-great, "I don't care what she calls you. You're still her granny."

. . .

Linda is a schoolteacher with children of her own, and every time she tries to remember the stories of her growing-up years, she forgets a family member or leaves out a funny little incident.

Then a couple of years ago during school Christmas vacation, as she tried to put together her family gift list, she decided that instead of coping with the crush of shoppers in order to give aunts and uncles another scarf or tie, she would deal with the rush of memory and bring back the sweetness of Christmas Past, the times they'd all spent together, the cousins and her own long-gone grandparents.

And so Linda sat down that very day and began to put together the memories of growing up. She wrote every day for three days about the things that—well, as she says, "You had to be there. If I tell you how funny it was when our dog chewed all the Christmas stockings, you probably wouldn't laugh."

Just days before the holiday, the books were finished. She titled them "Hello from Linda" and wrote a special dedication to each family member before she gift-wrapped and sent them.

Her father was the first to call. "Linda," he said, his voice choked with emotion, "I didn't even know you'd remember some of the things I'd already forgotten. This is the best present I ever had in my life."

"It turned out to be the best present I ever gave," Linda recalled, "because two weeks later without warning, without any sign of illness, Daddy died. I guess it was all made easier for me because I knew that even though I hadn't had the chance to say good-bye to him, I had had the chance to say hello."

NOT JUST A GREAT-GRANDMOTHER, BUT A REALLY GREAT GRANDMOTHER

There's a story going around my hometown about a man who decided to be a woman and two years ago began a series of operations. Today he is she.

To celebrate, he/she had a coming-out party given by—of all people—the woman to whom he/she was married.

A bit bizarre?

My son thought so when he told me.

My daughter said she'd always believed those kinds of stories were made up for TV talk shows.

But one person in our family simply shrugged and said, "That's how it is today. And it's fine. They're happy."

Of course the one person who accepted all this with equanimity is my mother, sometimes the oldest and sometimes the youngest of us all.

My mother and I, despite her age and mine, are still locked in that age-old mother/daughter relationship.

And so there are times when I feel that my

mother is the most terrific person in the world.

And there are times when she irritates me in ways no other person in the world does as she hovers over me still frowning and shaking her head over things I say and do.

Yet, despite her shortcomings (or are they mine?) I love her with a ferocity accorded few others in my life. I am her only child, and when she looks around at family gatherings, which now, thanks to marriage, remarriage, and the fecundity of succeeding generations, look like American Legion conventions, she marvels at how this all came as the result of one child.

She is in awe of the fact that she has lived to see her daughter's daughter's daughter. "I don't feel old," she explains, "until I say the number."

So, with true grandmotherly wisdom, she avoids saying the number. I think she's right. We set too much store by numbers and adjust expectations in accord. My mother thinks the expectations should not change with the numbers. High standards should not fall with succeeding birthdays.

Therefore, throughout my life she has been both supportive and critical, supportive always of my dreams and critical often of the way I have tried to realize them.

Still, whenever I confront her and her criticisms of me, she looks at me intently and says, "That's because I love you, Lois."

I am very sure of that.

And if we mothers and grandmothers let our children grow up secure in the knowledge that we love them, have we not fulfilled the chief role of mother, grandmother, and great-grandmother?

LOONY TUNES

Melanie is three years old, and she spends a large part of her day watching Loony Tunes.

Her talk is sprinkled with phrases like, "Goin' somewhere, Pigeon?"

Her mother, anxious to bring her daughter into the real world of duty and discipline, says frequently, "Melanie, life is not Loony Tunes."

Off to the side, Grandma listens and shakes her head.

She knows Melanie is absolutely right.

What is life if not Loony Tunes?

Exercise with Grandma

GRANDMA WEARS TIGHTS

f you want to take ten years off your body, just put on a black leotard or black tights.

Black hides black-and-blue (as in veins, spidery and otherwise) and tights hide loose (as in thighs and other parts of the body too disgusting to mention).

If you want to put on ten years, just go to a gym, look around, and see how some of those women (one or two of whom may be even older than you) can bend and stretch.

Still, for those of us who were never athletes, why should we now think that just because we've learned something along the way our muscles should also be newly educated and responsive to the latest aerobic exercise?

There was a time when I thought that if I went to exercise class, I would be inspired by the women around me, and pretty soon I'd be as proficient as they at bars and bells, dancing and prancing.

But to tell the truth, the best thing I ever got out of any exercise class was new friends.

57

You would never mistake Neil for the world's biggest four-year-old, so when he offered to help his dad take one of the kitchen chairs into the dining room, his father looked at him in surprise.

But sure enough, Little Neil flexed his muscles and moved the chair.

"How did you ever do that?" his mom asked in surprise.

"Well," he admitted sheepishly, "I've been lifting Grandma's weights."

Up to forty, it's all luck.
After forty, it's all maintenance.

Two three-year-olds were coming home in the nursery school car pool. Said one, "I am going to play at my grandma's."

Replied the second, "I can't. My grandma's at the gym."

. . . AND IN THE TWENTY-FIRST CENTURY

irls who were made of sugar and spice once dreamed of being nurses or teachers; boys set their sights on becoming doctors and firemen.

But that's not necessarily so for the twenty-first century.

I know of one granddaughter who wants to drive a truck, and my friend Pat's three-year-old grandson wants a tuxedo for his birthday so that he'll be properly dressed when he appears on stage playing the violin with the Philharmonic.

There is no beginning and no end to a child's dreams today.

My granddaughter Elizabeth has a friend whose parents are an attorney and a judge. In this case the daddy is the attorney, the mommy the judge.

One day at school the children in Elizabeth's class were asked what they wanted to be when they grew up.

One little boy announced that he wanted to be a judge.

Elizabeth laughed and laughed. "That's for

girls," she advised. "You should be a lawyer instead."

THE FOUR-YEAR-OLD IVY LEAGUE TRACK

Kathy, the most independent and self-sufficient of women, Kathy, the one who tries always to find her own way with the help of her husband and children, had fear in her voice when she called.

"I don't know what to do," she said, and I wondered what special miracle Kathy needed.

"It's Max," she explained. "I've applied to four schools for him."

"Wait a minute," I interrupted. "Max is only four, and you're applying to all these schools?"

"Yes, for next year. For kindergarten. I've investigated the public schools where we live, and we don't think they will challenge Max in the ways he should be challenged."

"So you're applying to private schools?"

"We have to," Kathy insisted.

I didn't debate that because, although I am a product of a fine public school system—as is my daughter—I know that all schools do not fill the needs of all children.

"Now here's the bad part," Kathy continued. "He's been turned down by one of the schools. We got the rejection letter today. And he loved this school. I took him there to visit, and he really liked the teachers and the playground."

"What about the other schools?"

"They could turn him down, too. Look, Mom, you have to understand something. If your child gets into the right school, then you can feel you're set for life. I mean, this is like the Ivy League track. You get him started right, and then life is all okay. I mean, I did everything right. I wore my little navy blue suit and pearls when I went for the interview, and I didn't look like a leftover hippie or somebody weird. And when they said they thought we might be an interesting family because Henry is an investigative reporter and I'm a writer, I even admitted that my mother is a writer, too. Now you know that if I'm willing to say I'm your daughter, I have to be pretty desperate."

I agreed. That is major desperation.

"I'll do what I can," I said fiercely. How could anyone turn down that adorable boy? How could anyone say no to our Max, the dear little boy his other grandmother calls The Poet? Max, with his soft eyes and sweet disposition and fine intelligence, not good enough for some dopey school?

In true grandmother fashion, I assumed automatically that the school must be shortsighted not to accept the brilliance of Max.

During the next days I talked to some of my friends in different cities with little children about to enter school. These mothers were as frantic as Kathy. One admitted that when she was interviewed by the school she wanted her child to attend, she had her skirt lengthened. "Look," she confided, "I don't want anyone who might take my child to think I have knees."

Another, fear in her voice, said, "When I got married, why didn't I make sure I was marrying into a legacy? You know, if your child has a parent who went to a private school, you're practically assured of a place. Why, oh why, did I marry a genius who only went to public school?"

Now, totally aware of the prevailing panic among the parents of four-year-olds, we made some calls.

As a result of our interference, Max did not get into any school where we used our so-called influence.

But, on his own and for all the right reasons, he was accepted at two schools that the family had wanted.

Two out of four.

Not bad in today's prep school sweepstakes.

But the anxiety hasn't ended.

In twelve years we'll have to face college.

INTERNATIONAL RELATIONS

American-born Bettina was visiting her English grandmother, and the two were window-shopping on Old Bond Street when seven-year-old Bettina noticed the taxicabs whizzing by. "Grandmother, what if . . ." she began, and then she hesitated.

"What if what?" Grandmother asked indulgently.

"Well, what if one of these cars came up over the curb and killed you? What would I do?"

"Oh dear," Grandmother exclaimed, "don't you know my address?"

"No."

"I live in Hempstead—or rather, since I'm now

Shopping
with
Grandma

dead, I used to live in Hempstead. Also, dear, remember that my full identification is in my handbag."

"Thank you, Grandmother," Bettina replied soberly. Suddenly her face brightened. "If you were dead, then there would be a funeral—"

"I suppose so."

"—and I'd be old enough to go," Bettina announced triumphantly.

Grandmother crossed the next block very carefully.

GRANDMA'S NIGHT OUT

Ian and Patsy are a country couple who don't socialize much. Their idea of a big night out is to go to the library and take out three books.

So, when Ian's brother announced that he was going to marry and have a big wedding, Ian and Patsy eagerly anticipated the social event of their season. Each day Ian came home with new details about the wedding.

One night he reported solemnly, "This wedding is so big that they're even going to invite your mother."

"Fantastic," said Patsy, who dearly loves her mother, and she promptly dialed Mama to tell her to watch for her invitation.

Sure enough, two weeks later the thick cream-colored invitation, with engraving so heavy you didn't even have to run your finger over it to make sure it was engraving, arrived at Grandma's. She called Patsy. "I got it," she announced proudly, "and I sent my acceptance."

"Good," her daughter replied. "We'll go together. Our invitation hasn't come yet, but you know how crazy the mails are. By the way, Allison will need a new dress for the wedding—"

"Oh, let me get it for her," Grandma interrupted. "I can just imagine what sweet things we'll find in toddler four."

Two days later Patsy called her mother, and even though it was a hot August day, there was a perceptible chill in Patsy's voice.

"A problem, dear?" her mother asked gently.

Experienced mothers with grown daughters know that they may or may not be the reason for a daughter's annoyance, so they play it safe and never ask a question with anything self-incriminating (e.g., "What did I do to annoy you?").

"Problem," Patsy choked. "Problem," she repeated hoarsely. "My problem is that my *darling* brother-in-law has decided that Allison will not go to the wedding. No children allowed. Did you ever—"

"No, I never," Grandma answered. It is always good politics to agree with an angry daughter, particularly when she is not angry with you.

"So look, Mom," Patsy said, her tone now becoming more gentle, "you'll have to sit."

"*Have* to sit?" Now it was Grandma's turn to be incensed. "But I've been invited. I've accepted."

"But you weren't invited for yourself," Patsy argued. "You were invited because of us."

"An invitation is an invitation," Grandma replied firmly.

"But I need you," her daughter moaned. "I need you to stay so I can go to my brother-in-law's wedding."

Grandma took a deep breath. "No," she said, "I'm not sitting."

"What kind of grandmother are you?" Patsy asked.

"A desirable one," her mother answered, "one who gets invited to family weddings and other parties, too. I'm also a grandmother who doesn't go back on her word. I will still buy Allison a wonderful party dress and take her for a special treat since *she* wasn't invited to the wedding."

. . .

In the end a sitter was hired, and all the grown-ups went to the wedding.

Will they all live happily ever after?

Grandma doesn't know about the bride and groom, but she's sure that she'll live happier in Ian and Patsy's world now that they understand that today's grandmothers are truly flexible.

They not only sit; they walk and run and dine and dance and attend weddings.

Go, Grandma!

THE VACATION PACKAGE

Veronica is one of those grandmothers with industrial-strength guilt.

Not to worry, her friends assure her.

We understand that you live five hundred miles from your grandchildren, so how can we expect you to be like us and give up everything in life to sit for them?

Relax, they say with a smile. We know that it's not a mortal sin if you don't visit grandchildren often. After all, you have a career (they say the word as if it were the newest disease), so how can you possibly pick up and fly to unimportant, dumb things like the school Grandmothers' Days and Christmas Whatevers?

And then Veronica's friends end with that real capper for the guilty granny, "Don't worry because you know how kids are. They'll probably love you more because they never see you."

Veronica nods at their reassurances and promptly dismisses everything they say. She doesn't believe them for a minute.

Veronica knows better.

She knows that if you want to see grandchildren, it's generally the grandparent who makes the move, not the family that has to pack and travel. So just this week Veronica decided she'd play the Grandmother Game in earnest.

She telephoned her travel agent and booked her family for a week at Disneyland.

"A week?" her daughter-in-law shrieked.

"What do you suggest?" Veronica asked carefully.

"Three days," her daughter-in-law promptly replied.

Miffed but not muted, Veronica said, "Four."

And so the family resolved to spend four days together in Disneyland.

"We're going to Disneyland," Veronica told all her friends, those friends who show the pictures and tell the stories about the children who "practically live at our house."

Ha ha, Veronica thought, wait until I show my Disneyland pictures with Mickey and Minnie.

Veronica's friends, however, were not particularly impressed with the prospect of the trip. And at lunch one day Veronica said to her best friend Judy, "Why don't the girls seem more excited about my going to Disneyland?"

Sighed Judy, "Because if you'd listened more

carefully, you'd know they've been there."

"To Disneyland?"

"No. To weekend, week-long family vacations."

"And?"

"And we all know they are fraught with danger."

"What kind of danger?"

"Look, Veronica," Judy said gingerly, "the girls love you, but they're afraid to tell you that after a family vacation Dora's son and daughter-in-law split. After a family vacation Joan's daughter became anorexic. After a family vacation Suzanne's brother-in-law changed his will and decided to leave all his money to charity instead of the kids, and—"

"Stop," Veronica said.

"As if that weren't enough," Judy said, "you can read a story in the papers about a woman who went on a Disneyland vacation with her family, got on the plane to go home, and attacked a stewardess. And it wasn't because of the rotten airline food."

"What was it?"

"A week with her family at Disneyland caused the poor dear to flip out. She was fined a thousand dollars, and she said it was worth it to get rid of the anger and frustration."

"Do you think I should cancel my trip?" Veronica asked.

"No," said Judy, "not until you find out whether that woman who attacked the stewardess was the mother or the grandmother."

HAVE I GOT A GRANDMOTHER FOR YOU

t was one of those marriages that's glued by children, cemented by debt, and held fast by tough times—only to fall apart in good times.

Sherry had always seen the signs of restlessness in her husband, and when Douglas realized that the children were out of the house for good, he decided to take off, too.

Their friends shook their heads and said they'd get back together, but Sherry knew they wouldn't. Douglas's idea of life was to become old and free; hers was to become old and even more close to family.

In the beginning Sherry was less stunned than sorrowful. How sad that Douglas didn't think grandfathering was as good as she considered grandmothering. In some ways, however, it was nice to have time on her hands again. Sherry took bridge lessons in the fall and tennis lessons in the spring. She thought about going on a trip that summer and considered a ski vacation for winter.

She was kind of proud of the way she could fill her days and nights. Every once in a while someone would tell her that Douglas had shown up here or there with a girl young enough to be his daughter, and she'd feel her stomach do the mambo. Men really were dumb.

"Why don't you meet someone and start going out, Mom?" her married daughter Monica asked one day.

Sherry laughed. "Right, dear. Women in their fifties are the latest sex symbols, aren't they? Don't you know what it's like out there? You think men are just waiting for the next available grandmother? Didn't you ever hear that old joke men always tell, 'I don't mind being a grandfather; what I can't stand is being married to a grandmother'?"

"All men aren't like that," her daughter assured her.

"They're not?" Sherry snapped. "Then find me a man."

"All right, just for that I will," her daughter retorted.

"It's not that your mother's bad-looking, and she's not dumb," Monica's husband said to his wife, "but guys aren't out looking in bars for grandmothers."

"And my mother isn't out there bar-hopping," Monica answered quickly. Then she added somewhat plaintively, "Does that mean that you mean you won't help me find a man for my mom?"

"Not *won't*," he assured her. "The word is *can't*."

Could it be true that her mother was right? If good, smart, honorable women couldn't meet men, what did that say for any woman's chances later in life?

"Maybe you ought to get a job," Monica told Sherry one day as they were shopping for a snowsuit for grandson Tony. "I'm not having too much luck finding a man."

"I told you," Sherry said. "Nobody wants a grandmother."

"Me wants grandmother," Tony piped.

Sherry turned to her three-year-old grandson.

"What did you say, honey?"

Tony looked at her with his big blue eyes. "I love you," he said with the innate wisdom of babyhood.

Sherry snapped her fingers. "That does it," she announced.

"What's 'it'?" Monica answered.

" 'It' is what Tony just told me. He told us who wants grandmothers. Kids want grandmothers, and mothers need grandmothers. Monica, you've been after me to get a job, and I don't want to stand behind some ribbon counter in a discount store selling people I don't like things they don't need. You know what I'm going to do instead? I'm going to get two retired teachers who live on my street and the nurse who's a widow, and I'm going to start a little day care center."

"You do that, and I'll get you all the business you can possibly handle," her daughter assured her.

"I do believe you can, dear," Sherry answered.

When Monica told her husband, he nodded approvingly. "I'll name your mom's business," he said. "Tell her to call it 'Have I Got a Grandmother for You.'"

Within a year Sherry had her business up and

running. And, for the first time, when she heard about the girls her ex-husband was seeing, she shrugged. Who cared? She had her own life and her own interests.

One day one of the mothers whose child was at Sherry's school asked if her mother might come to observe, and that gave Sherry the idea to have a Grandmothers Day. "The next time," one granny suggested, "include grandpas, too." And a year later Sherry welcomed contemporaries to the center's first Grandparents Day.

And as one of the mothers introduced her son's grandfather, the grandfather said in a low voice, "Hello, gorgeous."

She looked into his eyes. No, no. It had been at least a thousand years since high school and Norman—

She took her head slowly. "Norman?"

"You never forget an old boyfriend, do you, Sherry?"

"How could you possibly recognize me?" she asked, touching her short frosted hair.

"Because you still walk like you jitterbug," he laughed. "You always leaned a little to the left. I just didn't know who my grandson's beloved Miss Sherry was. Tell me, what's going on in your life, because who knows? Have I Got a Grandmother for You may turn out to be a blessing for grand-fathers, too."

Sherry and Norman saw a lot of each other that winter, and in the spring widower Norman and divorcee Sherry decided to try marriage one more time.

And, as Sherry admitted to Monica, "I guess this all proves that grandmothers *can* get married—provided they meet grandfathers."

SEX AND THE SINGLE GRANDDAUGHTER

She suffers, as do many contemporary grandchildren, from being seven in a world where seventeen seems like a lot more fun. If only she knew—well, she doesn't—so here we are with this little girl in braces and pinafores yearning for rock and roll instead of a pet rock and some jelly roll.

No, her mother has told her again and again, you are too young to have your ears pierced. No, she has been told, you cannot stay up until nine o'clock because if you do, you are impossible for three days.

So what is a girl to do?

There is just one answer. Visit her grandmother.

And that's how Theresa came to visit Grandma for a sleepover carrying her tube of colorless lipstick, her tape player, and a black body stocking. She also had, at her mother's insistence, a toothbrush, a hairbrush, and a library book.

"Grandma, what time do I have to go to bed?" Theresa asked.

"Whenever you like, dear."

"Grandma, can I put on your jewelry?"

"Of course, dear."

"Grandma, is it OK if I watch television?"

"Certainly."

Grandma chuckled. Her daughter always thought Theresa was at a difficult age. How silly. All the little girl needed was a little yessing in that world of no.

So it came to happen that at 11 P.M., when Grandma poked her head into the room where Theresa was supposedly sleeping, there was Theresa in the middle of the bed drinking a soft drink, eating potato chips, and clicking the TV channel selector with kidlike excitement and teenlike impunity.

"What are you watching?" Grandma asked, pleased to be the agent of her granddaughter's adventure.

"I just keep changing channels and looking," the little girl answered blithely. "See, isn't it fun?" and Theresa whizzed past a football game, a tennis match, soccer in Australia, and suddenly stopped. "Wow!" she gasped. "What's that?"

Grandma almost fell out of her red high heels as she saw a nearly naked couple embracing. "That," said Grandma, recovering her balance and her words quickly, "is an ad for underwear. It's really disgusting. Look how fat she is." And then Grandma, full of guilt and nervous reaction, reached over and switched channels. Well, what else could she have said or done? Certainly she knew that she never should have made fun of a fat woman. But who ever expected that bare-bosomed woman to turn up in the guest bedroom performing for her granddaughter? Good God, Theresa had found one of those adult film channels. You could have them zapped from your set, but when you're an adult living alone, why would you even think about that?

"Grandma," Theresa asked, "have you ever seen an X-rated movie?"

Grandma jumped. How did little innocent Theresa know that term? Had she understood what she'd just seen? Would she tell her mother she and Grandma sat up late and watched porno movies? Grandma pasted a smile on her frozen face. "No, I never have."

Theresa sighed. "You're just like my mother. She never saw one either. I figured you would have, and you'd tell me about it."

"Sorry," said Grandma as she stumbled backward from the bedroom and reached for the telephone. Her daughter was still awake. "I have an apology," Grandma mumbled. "You're right. Raising children isn't the way it was. We only had protests and delinquency and truancy and dropping out and cults. We didn't have film ratings and drugs and AIDS. I hope you don't mind, darling, but I'm sending Theresa home early tomorrow."

YOU CAN FOOL SOME OF THE GRANDCHILDREN SOME OF THE TIME . . .

he grandkids coming to dinner tonight?" Grandpa Harry asked when he saw the table set for six.

"Yes." Grandma Ellen smiled.

"What are you making?"

"Grandma food. Brisket, little potatoes, applesauce."

"In that case," Grandpa confided, "I'm going to fool the kids."

"What does that mean?" Grandma asked with the wariness of a woman who knows from experience that a man's fooling is sometimes a synonym for a man's foolishness.

"You'll see," Grandpa chortled.

They were halfway through the brisket on the way to applesauce overkill when Grandpa turned to Daisy. "You know what that meat is?" he asked the eight-year-old.

"Brisket," she replied swiftly.

"No," Grandpa laughed, "that's dinosaur meat."

Daisy rolled her eyes in exasperation. Gee

whiz, didn't Grandpa know that dinosaurs were extinct even before grandmothers made briskets?

"And see those little round things?" Grandpa chuckled, pointing to the small white potatoes.

"Uh huh," the eight-year-old replied.

"They're whale eggs," Grandpa announced with a twinkle at everyone else at the table.

Daisy put her fork down. "They are not whale eggs," she said forcefully. "Whales are mammals, and they do not lay eggs. You are making a common mistake because you probably think mammals, like fish, are cold-blooded vertebrates. Whales are warm-blooded and nurse their young—"

"I know, I know," Grandpa answered petulantly.

Some hours later he turned to Grandma. "What's with these kids?" he asked. "How come our grandchildren have no sense of humor? Our kids always laughed when I did the whale egg and dinosaur jokes."

"Harry," Grandma explained carefully, "you have missed the point of this new generation."

"What's that?"

"The terrible truth is that these little kids have smart parents, and our poor kids didn't."

SWIM FOR YOUR LIFE, GRANNY

There isn't much that frightens me any longer.

I have been inches from elephants while on safari in Africa. I've been in tough neighborhoods with even tougher characters, and I've had more white-knuckle flights than most grandmothers.

So what makes me break out in a cold sweat at this time in life?

Only one thing.

Buying a bathing suit.

The thought of taking my aging body to teenage heaven, the dressing room in the swimsuit department, is my idea of being in deep water.

Fully dressed, most of us can get away with a lot and hide the flaws that Mother Nature reveals.

But put us, bare-legged and almost naked under those yellow lights and in front of those tell-all mirrors, and you show me the over-forty who can be vain about veins.

Indeed, what woman of any age can ignore the cheesecake thighs, the too-dimpled knees, the rolling valleys where once there were hills?

Over the years I've read the beauty pages and tried to take the hints: a skirted suit hides the thighs; black reduces the overall size of practically anything that's bigger than a family-size refrigerator; one-piece suits are made for hiding it all while bikinis and two-piece suits let it all hang out.

But no matter which kind of swimsuit I buy, it still doesn't hide the most of me, which I wish were the least of me. The only solution is never to wear a bathing suit, or to wear any bathing suit I want and stay in the water with the grandchildren all the time.

I know there's another road, but I've been unwilling to take it: the nip-and-tuck route to swimsuit stardom.

While I uphold the rights of women to remake themselves in any way they want, I do withhold my approval when it comes to plastic surgery. If it's surgery performed because of an accident or birth defect, I wholeheartedly approve.

But if alterations are made to satisfy a husband who wants a wife/toy, to "recover" from a divorce, or to meet unreal expectations of media beauty standards, I draw the line.

Do women who go trotting off to plastic surgeons believe that you're only as popular as your body?

Do they honestly think that grandmas are a category in the Miss America swimsuit competition? Or that a measured body is a treasured one?

Do they still think that sweater girls are better girls?

Getting older isn't the worst thing that can happen to us grandmothers; not having the opportunity to age is the bitter alternative. Why should we expect the broken veins, the stretch marks, the detritus of childbearing to get better with the years? Isn't it about time that we altered our self-perception of body instead of bobbing and adding here and there?

Why should we succumb to the ads that offer the services of a plastic surgeon who promises every woman a beautiful bosom?

Where, oh where, is the ad that promises us we will be cherished for the love we give, the kindnesses we bestow, the generous spirit that pervades our lives?

When will the fiction that we women help create for ourselves be supplanted by the truth?

Maybe we can all begin to think the truth about

our bodies and ourselves when we walk into the dressing room to buy a bathing suit this year, and instead of giving in to the sadness of looking at a body that has moved in old directions we'll be grateful instead for a mind that has moved in new ones.

And maybe, just maybe, we can persuade those men who don't yet get the message that an uplifted bosom doesn't guarantee an uplifting life and that a firm behind does not portend a firm future for us—or our grandchildren.

YOU WON'T BELIEVE WHAT MY GRANDCHILD SAID

N o one stops to listen to what your grandchild said, which is why this is a collection to read:

Suzannah, age four, was visiting a friend for a slumber party. "However did they find space for you in that tiny apartment?" her grandmother asked.

"Oh, they had plenty of room," Suzannah assured her. "I slept on a crouton."

Sophisticated and sure of herself, six-year-old Melissa told her grandmother that she not only knew how to have babies, she knew how not to have babies.

"Really?" asked Grandma. "How?"

"You go to the drugstore," Melissa advised, "and you buy a condo."

Four-year-old Gail was sitting quietly as her parents fussed over Gil, her five-year-old brother.

Grandmother, noticing how quiet the usually effervescent Gail had become said, "Oh, Gail, we're all excited about Gil because he got into such a fine school. Next year when you're accepted at kindergarten we'll be proud of you, too."

Gail stood, slapped her hand against her forehead, and moaned, "Talk about pressure."

THE FIRST DAY OF CHRISTMAS

And it came to pass that Max, kindergarten pupil par excellence, called to say that he was going to be in the school Christmas program.

So what is a grandmother to do?

That's easy to figure.

She'll board the quickest train and head for the hills where the *Wunderkind*, wearing a red bow tie and blue blazer as well as shoes that bear no resemblance to the daily high-tops, will raise his voice in holiday song.

Never mind that travel time will be three hours, that the program, kindergarten through grade five, will go on for thirty minutes, that Grandmother has a preholiday schedule that fills two date books—Grandmother will be on hand.

Max awoke sensitive to the pressures of stardom. In his natty attire he could barely control his excitement as he wolfed his morning oatmeal. "Careful," his mother cautioned, "or you'll get your shirt dirty."

Immediately he spattered his oatmeal on his shirt. "Mommy," he cried, "why did you have to say that? See what you made me do."

"I'll change your shirt," Mommy volunteered.

"Just clean me up," he mumbled.

When the bus arrived, Max was waiting in front of his house.

"Don't forget to look for me at the program," he reminded his mother.

"I'll try to remember," his mother promised.

The auditorium was decorated with branches, a Christmas tree, and a Chanukah menorah— the ecumenical signs of the season.

And when Max saw his parents and grand- mother enter the auditorium, he jumped from his chair and waved wildly, an ear-to-ear grin on his face.

"See? He's glad you came," his mother said to his grandmother.

"Glad *I* came?" Grandmother questioned. "He doesn't even see me."

"It's okay anyway," Mommy said reassuringly to her mother.

The program was dear.

Little children stood and told their definition of miracle. (Example: Your father says you can't ever have a dog, and you find a dog on the front porch. That is a miracle!)

Came time for the kindergarten portion, and Grandmother strained to see Maxie walk up onstage. But the kindergarten sat still, and then Grandmother realized that for his first public appearance, Max would not command center stage but would perform *in situ*.

The class turned around in their seats, faced the back of the auditorium, where the nervous parents and anxious grandparents sat, and sang their song. It was one of those songs with gestures, and with Daddy taping the full show, Max did a splendid job of putting his head on his hands to simulate the baby in the manger. Grandmother could not identify Max's voice as they sang "Oh Come Little Children," but this she knew—he definitely moved his lips.

Later, as Grandmother reflected on the mad dash to school and the program that ensued, she realized that someday Max may read a significant scientific paper or sing madrigals in odea the world over—but chances are that he will never thrill an audience as he did his parents and grandmother at his school debut in the Christmas program.

CHILD OF MY CHILD

Oh, child of my child,
Hope of my hopes,
Dream of my dreams.
You are born of my past
En route to your future.

Even though
You will learn
What I only imagined,
Experience
What I only supposed,
Grow wise
In things I only guessed,
Let me share this
Space and place
With you.

. . .

Only then can I trust the future
I will not live to see.
For no matter what riches

I amass in the world,
You, the child of my child,
Are my truest legacy.

Over the hills and through the woods to Grandmother's condo we go

THE PREFAB GRANDMOTHER, CIRCA 1990S

he first time my granddaughter Josie met me she came to dinner in her "Sweeping Beauty dwess," put her arms around me, and told me she was going to "wuv Gwandma Wowis."

Josie was three at the time, and I was in need of all the "wuv" I could get because I was walking into the role of new grandmother with a new husband in a new city.

Like so many women, I have come to grandmotherhood both on my own and with the help of others. We who have both married and remarried can tell the world more about mergers and acquisitions than any Wall Street trader.

My eighteen grandchildren come from eight children, only two of whom were born to me. The rest were reborn to me. Some of them were so young (or unborn) when I assumed the grandmother role that they think I was born to them.

My husband thinks we are natural-born grandparents, and that's probably a very good thing, considering he's been at it since the age of forty-five.

Still, most people look at our large brood and cluck compassionately. They wonder how we can stand the noise.

Answer: We don't. We get all the family together only a couple of times a year. At other times we keep the group down to a manageable twenty or so adults and children.

Another concern people voice: How do we remember the birthdays?

Answer: I don't; Bud does. He carries a copy of everybody's birthdate on a list in the front of his datebook, and each month he marks the days we have to remember.

The third question we get is: How can you remember what to say to each child?

Answer: Just say "yes," and what grandchild won't love you?

WATCH OUT. GRANDMA'S IN THE KITCHEN.

Although one of my friends says the newest thing in grandmothers' apartments is no kitchen, I don't agree. Kitchens kind of run in my family. We've always had one, each an appliance better than the one that preceded it.

So, when Bud and I moved into our new all-on-one-floor grandparent-style apartment, I immediately announced what I wanted in a kitchen, all of which can be summed up with

More of—

Better than—

Lots of—

So New Kitchen, instead of featuring one oven that holds a thirty-pound turkey, has two.

Griddle in the middle? Must have.

Supersize burners? Light my fire.

Corner cabinets? No angle overlooked.

Special lighting? The better to see the color of the food.

The new microwave is so talented that you don't have to rotate the food.

The two sinks have two dishwashers.

There are file drawers for recipes clipped,

Cooking Lessons with Grandma

JOE'S PIZZERIA we deliver call us

shelves to hold cookbooks.

There is a wine cooler for lifting low spirits, a ladder for soaring to new cabinet heights.

By the time the kitchen was finished, it looked too good for cooking.

But cooking is what kitchens are about, so after the last box was unpacked, I announced to my beloved that we would have dinner at home, dinner *à deux*. Just an ordinary pot roast by candlelight. Well, not exactly pot roast. I would broil some fish.

What a kitchen! I sliced and diced by the light of the silvery counter.

To practice the broiling technique with the new oven with a brain, I decided to roast some no-brainer peppers.

In went the peppers, on went my glasses, and the oven and I engaged in the serious business of becoming friends. I patted the shiny surface. "I know you're user friendly," I assured the oven.

Look, if you can talk to plants, why not ovens?

I took a deep breath and pressed the tempera-ture button once (that's what it says in the book). If you press twice, everything goes off, and noth-ing will ever happen. Sure enough, one push, one twirl of the time/temperature button, and a flurry of little digital numbers appeared. Numbers? I wanted old-fashioned broil. At last *brl* came on the screen. I felt waves of relief. I would brl to my heart's content. I opened the door, put in my peppers, closed the door, and waited. Nothing happened. Oops, I'd forgotten the child-proof safety switch. I smiled. Grandmothers certainly need to be child-proofed. "I've got your secrets now," I said, wagging a cautious finger at the oven. Then I set the timer for five minutes and walked away.

Five minutes later there was a siren screaming in the kitchen. The timer was calling to me. My new friend, my dear oven, was calling to tell me my peppers were done.

I crossed the kitchen in a flash, pushed the button twice, and threw the safety switch to open the oven door.

I pulled the handle.

Nothing happened.

I pulled and I tugged.

Still nothing happened, but I knew the peppers inside were continuing to make a statement.

Now I just started pushing any button I could find.

Still nothing.

I had visions of peppers growing old and cold in that oven.

"Bud," I called frantically.

My hero came running in.

"I can't turn off the oven."

"Read the book."

"I did."

He sniffed. "Then what's cooking?"

"Peppers."

"I thought you were broiling fish."

"Later. First, please rescue my peppers."

"I'll throw the breaker," he said firmly.

"You'll do what?" I shrieked.

"Turn off the breaker," he explained slowly. "It will make the electricity go off so that the oven door will open, and you can start all over again."

"Let me tell you about this kitchen," I said to Bud at 10 P.M. when we sat down to dinner. "It is really very beautiful. But someone should rush right over and photograph it before I broil it in two ovens along with sixty pounds of turkey. I am the newest kind of victim in the world of victimization. I am the victim of technology. Someday our grandchildren will get new ranges and say to their spouses, 'Just look what they finally invented—a range that has the words *bake* and *broil* so that all you do is turn a knob. And to get the right temperature you set a dial—and you can see the numbers all at once.'"

"DEAR GRANDMA . . .

t was really great to see you over the Thanksgiving holiday. Well, Grandma, to tell the truth, it wasn't great. Not that I don't love you. I do love you, Grandma, but I've got a problem with my family, and if you can help, I'd really appreciate it a lot.

Grandma, my parents act like they think I'm still seven years old, and they're still dividing me the way they've been ever since the divorce. I know you're Mom's mom, so you're going to say I should spend more time with Mom, but Grandma, honest, Mom isn't giving me love. She's giving me headaches.

Look, Grandma, my father and his wife aren't perfect either. That's my problem. If I had just one perfect parent, I'd be OK.

But here's what happened to me Thanksgiving weekend. My parents told me I'd have to give 50% of my time to my mother and 50% of my time to my father. But I also needed 50% for home-work, 50% for my girlfriend, and 25% for the rest of my friends.

Maybe you can help my mom understand and stop pushing me. Maybe you can make my dad listen to you because he doesn't really have to. Maybe you can show them both this letter.

All I know, Grandma, is that I'm going to my roommate's for Christmas break. He's an orphan.

Love you,
Ned"

SUPER GRANNY

hey don't wait for me at the door of the supermarket each August, but I think they should because when August comes, so do my grandchildren, and the way I buy out the supermarket shelves for those nine kids, you'd think I was expecting the Big Bang.

In the beginning, back when we began cele-brating the girls' birthdays in August, I would make lists and buy intelligently. And then I learned that there is no method that guarantees that what a child liked last year, he or she will like this year. So now I'm reduced to wild-card buying. I just race up and down the aisles as though I'm one of those winners on a TV show who has seventeen minutes to spend a million dollars. Like a shopping nut, I reach thither and yon, and when one basket is full, I race back for another.

My shopping is done in stages. I begin with the nonperishables and buy them two weeks in advance of the arrival of the families.

The usual first stop is the juice shelves. Everybody drinks juice out of a box. It's OK with me. It does keep the dishwasher loads down, but I know that for weeks I'll stumble over half-consumed dripping boxes with little plastic straws. But look. This is what my babies want; this is what my babies get. And so I buy a dozen apple juices, and then I pause. Does Elizabeth drink apple? No, I think she's the one who likes cranberry. Woosh! Here comes a dozen cranberry. But Stephanie didn't like cranberry, did she? But forget Stephanie's preferences because she'll drink black mud if Marisa thinks it's best. So what does Marisa like? Hmmmmm. Maybe grape. OK. A dozen grape. That's for Marisa. Now add a dozen for Stephanie. And then remember that Marisa eats more than Stephanie. Means she probably drinks more, too.

Twelve more, and here's looking at you, Marisa dear. Oh oh, almost forgot the M&M grandchildren. What do Max and Molly want? Probably something different. Throw in a dozen apple/cranberry for each. Alex—what would Alex want? Doesn't matter because I've never seen Alex eat. Does Alex eat?

I forge ahead. Here we are at cereals. OK. Loops for one, and O's for another. Add a little flakes and crisp and stick it all together with some honey on the side.

Can't forget the peanut butter and jelly. Who're the creamies, and who are the chunkies? Can't remember. Better get six jars of each. Plus a jar of grape jelly, raspberry preserves, strawberry preserves. Doesn't look like enough. Throw in another of each.

Pick up two big detergent boxes because once the grandchildren arrive, the bell rings and the house goes on rinse cycle. Mustn't forget the bleach and the fabric softener.

Cookies. Brownie mix. Chocolate syrup. Let's see. What else would their parents not want them to have?

Well, this will do for starters.

On the way out I see a woman who looks as

old as I feel. She is pushing a cart, and there is a small child sitting in her basket. "Grandmother?" I ask.

She nods.

"Did you just buy out the store, too?"

"Did I buy out the store?" she asks in answer to my question. "I buy like I never bought before. After my children grew up, my food bills were about a hundred dollars a week for my husband and me. Now each weekend that a grandchild comes to visit, my bills go to three hundred a week."

"Do they eat that much?"

She eyes my basket suspiciously. "It's not that they are such big eaters. It's just that"—now she looks at my three overflowing baskets of junk—"I buy the best. Lamb chops and chicken, but only the best. I make soup."

I try to hide my instant brownie mix packages. "Ummmmm," I try to explain, "this isn't everything I'm going to buy. I ordered a sixteen-pound turkey breast, and we're going to barbecue and have parties and eat a lot."

She does not look as if she believes me.

"Honestly," I try to explain. "This is just for starters."

She sniffs suspiciously and clutches her grandchild tightly. No use letting her lamb chop princess get too close to a peanut butter grandmother like me.

Of course, as it all turned out, I'd bought all the wrong amounts. I was so worried that we might run out of mustard (mustard!) that I bought six jars, which are still gathering dust on my top shelves. I overbought juice boxes, underestimated milk.

Along the way I also bought wire baskets for all the children, lined them with face cloths and towels, and wrote each child's name on a basket so that wherever they slept, they'd always have towels and underwear at hand. The mothers were all very complimentary about my foresight, thought it a great idea. The only problem was that the children never went from barn to house carrying their baskets as we expected them to.

But there were other unexpected parts, too. Alex didn't come; he decided to stay at home with his dad, who was working that weekend. Baby Emily stayed with them, too, and Denise and Stephanie had a wonderful mother-daughter holiday and made plans for a separate holiday with

Heidi and her daughters the next summer.

So after all that shopping, what did the kids vote as best dinner?

The night they went to the fast-food restaurant down the street and came back to watch a rented movie.

THE FIRST GRANDMOTHER

Hannah took a brightly colored string, tied six balloons together, and put them on a table.

It wasn't part of her job as concierge, of course, but this was New Year's Eve, and the hotel staff was always slightly frenzied at holiday time, and she knew that extra hands were needed. So she had come into the dining room, as she had for so many years, to help the others.

In the beginning she'd thought busy work would make her forget about New Year's Eve, the holiday she most dreaded. But each year she found that, much as she wanted to throw off the past, it was still a time when she remembered—

Ach, what was the difference what she remembered?

So many years now since all was gone. Gone with that long-ago war. Who still remembered that there was a time when German children did not live beyond a certain age, and if they did—

—And if they did, then they were orphans. Orphans of the Holocaust.

Hannah was one of those Holocaust children, a lucky one. Or so people said. But often she had wondered. Was it good luck or bad? What kind of luck had sent her to England to be raised by a distant cousin while her parents and grandparents and aunts and uncles stayed in Europe, only to die—all of them—in the crematorium in Poland?

Still, she had survived because her father had said the family must not die out; she would live for all of them. And so she had. She knew that most people would call that luck.

She had married. Yes, she would live for all who died.

But her marriage was to end in tragedy when her husband was killed in a traffic accident on a London street. She was already pregnant with Gary when it happened.

The young widowed mother went to work and raised Gary with the double duty of a fatherless son. He was both the child who obeyed the mother and the man of the house. Hannah never married again.

Gary went to university, became an architect, and now—now after all his years of scrimping and working, finally seemed to have a solid footing with his career.

Even the rest of his life was in balance. Three years ago, at the age of thirty-seven, he married Hillary, a woman his age.

Good and bad in the marriage, Hannah thought.

A woman old enough to be a wife, but was she too old to be a mother?

Was Hannah to have survived only to let those who had died before her have no one left to bear the legacy of their talents?

"Do you want children?" she had asked Hillary.

"Perhaps," she'd answered.

But Gary had told her they were trying to have a family of their own.

There were two miscarriages.

And then six months ago they had come to the hotel to have dinner with Hannah and tell her that Hillary was in her second trimester. The child was due the last week in December. Each day now she awoke with a sense of fear—would there be another child—would all of this ever make any kind of sense?

Then this morning Gary had called to say that Hillary was going into labor.

"I'll be at work," she'd said, "because I am too nervous to stay at home, too frightened to be at hospital with you—"

"I will find you," her son promised.

Hannah tied another balloon cluster.

She looked at her watch. In a few hours this room would be filled with cheering, happy people. Would she be one of them?

Where was Gary's call?

She reached for another balloon string and felt a hand on hers.

She looked up. "Gary."

"It's a boy, Mama."

She let a small sob escape, a sob of relief and joy.

"You see, Mama," Gary said as he put his arm around her. "This is why your parents saved you from the Holocaust."

"Yes," she said kissing her son, "and I can give

your son something you never had, a grandmother. Do you realize, my son, that in our family I
am the first grandmother in three generations?"

THE GRANNIES WHO LUNCH

he first time that a child learns that lunch
can be more than a peanut butter sandwich is the day his grandmother takes
him to lunch.

When I was a child, and when my children
were children, the grandmother treat lunch was
to go to a department store, and there amidst the
determinedly cheerful decor of a restaurant
within the store, grandmother and grandchild
would be served by a starched and polite woman
of uncertain years the specialties that even now
cause waves of gastronomic nostalgia: chicken
pot pie, turkey club sandwich, Welsh rarebit ("No,
dear, Grandma promises you that it's not Peter
Rabbit you're eating"), and such grand desserts
as Miss Charlotte's Pecan Pie or Butterscotch
Nut Ball.

How can today's lunches—pizza on the run,
hamburger on a bun—compare to the delicious

golden tastes of those times?

Yet despite the accelerated schedules, the abbreviated menus, and the disappearance of those old-style grandmother restaurants (remember Schrafft's and Stouffer's?), grandmothers and grandchildren still manage to break bread together.

One grandmother stopped at the neighborhood mall with her two grandchildren: a four-year-old boy and a three-year-old girl. As they were eating around the crusts of their pizzas, their grandmother asked (a favorite grandmother trick to get grandchildren to love them), "Now who wants ice cream for dessert?"

Mother nudged Grandmother and said quietly, "Grandmother, you mean y-o-g-u-r-t."

"Ha," piped the four-year-old, wise to his mother's ways. "That spells 'no way.'"

The line was full of eager young things waiting to order hamburgers and fries when suddenly a grown woman elbowed her way to the front and shouted to the beleaguered man behind the counter, "You forgot the treat in my Happy Box."

The children looked in amazement at the grown woman who wanted her kid prize until she turned to them, hands on hips, and asked, "You think I want my grandson to kill me?"

Granny looked at the menu and asked Roseanne if she would like a hamburger with fries or a chicken sandwich for lunch.

Roseanne shook her red curls. "I don't want that kind of food," she answered. "You see, Granny, my stomach is divided in two parts. There is a part for meat and a part for desserts. The part for meat is always full, and the part for desserts can always eat more. So if you don't mind I'll just have some brownies and cookies and ice cream."

FUTURES

In the dreams
Of children
Are the hopes
Of grandparents.

FRANCO-AMERICAN STYLE

*H*er grandfather came from Alsace after the War of 1870, and not only did he leave a leafy family tree of four children but he practically reforested two continents, for he then proceeded to have five children in the United States. These children, in turn, produced more than one hundred great-great-greats and greater-yets.

Marie, one of the greater-yets in the United States, was determined—once she became a granny—that the new generation in each country must not grow up unaware of their dual legacy, and so she contacted one of her cousin contemporaries in Paris.

"Do you suppose that you and I might plan an international family reunion?" she asked.

"Has it ever been done?" her French cousin asked.

"Not in our family," was the answer.

So the two cousins, like the experienced businesspersons they both are, decided to cochair the event. The cousin in Paris was European chairman; Marie, the American chair.

It took two years of planning, but 108 cousins came to Baltimore for the first reunion, and few came empty-handed.

The cousins in charge decided that the only gifts that would be acceptable for the family would be the gifts of self, so each person was encouraged to do something that would help the new and long-distance cousins appreciate his or her talents.

One cousin, a printer, made a family tree for each attendee. Another, a musician, made a tape of Alsatian music. A minister cousin gave the invocation. The local cousins all contributed the food from their kitchens. And from the small town in Alsace and from Baltimore, where they met, came proclamations from the mayors.

And what was the result of the first reunion?

One stepgrandchild became a close friend of a French grandchild, and the two have since traveled together.

All the cousins are so enchanted with their relationship that they have agreed that the family will reunite every five years.

Said Marie, the grandmother who started it all, "We all wonder what we are going to leave our children and our grandchildren. I feel good because I think I just may have given all my children and my children's children their history, and that is really something to remember me by."

CURTAIN GOING UP

My children were raised on a rich diet of make-believe. They went to the theater from the time they were old enough to sit up, and I've always hoped that somehow things would work out so that I might be there when this newest television generation was introduced to the thrill of seeing real, live actors.

And then one day I heard that *Peter Pan* was about to reenter children's hearts at a theater near us. I called Kathy to see if I might rent her children for an afternoon of major theater going.

In true good mom fashion she 1) said yes, and 2) prepped her children for a week in advance of our theater date by feeding them daily doses of the *Peter Pan* tape of the Mary Martin version.

When Max and Molly came to the city, their excitement was as nothing compared to mine.

They understood that this was not going to be

a film version of their story, but still they weren't quite sure what live theater was. The theater was filled with maybe a million squirming kids and six parents and grandparents. We made our way to our seats, center of the house, eighth row. Indeed, they were perfectly fine seats until two ten-year-old giants sat in front of us. I clenched my teeth.

I knew the complaining would begin.

Max looked around Giant Number One from the right and then the left. He pursed his little lips, and then with the wisdom of a four-year-old who's played with bigger kids, he simply took his coat, folded it, and sat on top of it. And he didn't say a word.

Molly, unaware of her brother's accommodation to the human roadblocks, adjusted herself until she sat on her knees and had her own good view. And she didn't say a word.

All this was before the play began.

When the lights in the theater were lowered and the theater darkened, each child looked anxiously at me. "It's all right," I explained. "This is the way all plays begin. The lights all go down before the curtain goes up. What's the curtain? That big cloth that's hiding the stage. See?"

Funny the way grandparents forget what kids have yet to learn.

From the moment the Darling children spoke, my darling grandchildren were captivated. All around us children squirmed, coughed, squealed, and talked. Not my kids. They never said a word, but gazed in silent fascination at the stage.

At the end of Act I, Max turned. "Is that the end, Grandma?"

"No," I assured him. "You know the story. There's more to come. We still have to see the pirates."

"I knew that," Molly said. Molly at three didn't miss much.

"Then why did they stop the play?" Max asked.

"Because," I explained, "you know the way it is on television. Every once in a while they stop the show so that the station can run commercials. Well, this is the theater's commercial, and they sell candy. Want to get candy?"

Both Max and Molly thought that was a very good idea. We went to the candy counter, muscled our way past some tough-looking six-year-olds, and got ourselves a few chocolate commercials to get us through Act II.

As we walked home, I thought about all the theater I've seen. I thought about the time I took Max and Molly's mother to see *Peter Pan*, and she held a lucky ticket, was brought up onstage, and actually flew like Peter Pan. I thought about the times I've been to London, the opening nights I've attended in New York. I thought about Paris and Venice and Vienna, all the places and times I've been in the most wonderful theaters in the world, and I thought that as magical as the theater is, there is nothing like the first time the curtain goes up, and a whole new world is opened to you forever.

GRANDMOTHERS IN SICKNESS AND IN HEALTH

Annabelle made up her mind that she was going to get right into it with her grandchildren on this visit. They'd come and play outside, and she would, too. They'd run and jump and rollerskate, and she would, too.

Indeed, she reminded herself, what's the point of being vital and young and grandmotherly if you didn't act vital and young but only grand-motherly?

So when the four children arrived, Annabelle skipped with them in the winter sun and took them skating. She played tag and hide-and-seek and ran around the big yard under the maples. And when the children left, they agreed that Grandmom was the best.

Next day, Annabelle called Mommy so she could hear how much fun the children had. "Oh, it really was wonderful, and they loved playing with you," was the report, and then there was a long pause, "—but today they all have strep throats."

Grandmom Annabelle knew she was sup-posed to sympathize, but instead she admitted, "Come to think of it, I don't feel so hot either." By afternoon her temperature was higher than the Dow Jones Index.

After forty-eight hours, Annabelle in a croaking half-whisper checked in to see how the children were doing and learned that they were healthy and back in school. "Just one of those usual kid things that comes and goes," was the word from Mommy.

Two weeks later Annabelle was still coughing and sniffling when the grandchildren called to say, "We had so much fun we want to come again."

"Not until my temperature goes down," Annabelle moaned. "I can run and jump like a kid. I just can't recuperate like one."

I know what Annabelle means.

We had been away in the Caribbean, had a picture postcard vacation and then, the day before we were to come home and prepare for a next-day visit from three of the grandchildren, I fell in a hole and broke my ankle in two places.

Broken bones are an everyday thing with some of our grandchildren. Indeed, as daughter Lee said, "We thought Lindsay had the corner on the broken-bone market; we didn't know you could do it, too."

Over the weeks that followed I learned about wheelchairs and crutches. As I struggled with the crutches, people would often stop me (it was very easy to stop me) and say, "Oh, you'll get the hang of those in a few days. I know because I broke my leg when I was seventeen, and I had to use crutches, too."

Ha ha. That was my answer.

There are some things in life that are even

beyond a grandmother, and being an agile seventeen is one of them.

FOREIGN AFFAIRS

f it's two minutes to July, Colleen is about to play grandmom again because once a year her son, an engineer in South America, returns to the United States with his wife and four children. During that once-a-year time, Colleen and Herb collect all the grandchildren from their six children and take a month mixing and matching families.

"I spend a lot of time in the pediatrician's office," she confesses, "because my South American family saves up their sniffles and shots for Grams. But that isn't the problem. Our big question is where shall we rent for the month?

"Herb and I live in an apartment, and, of course, it's not big enough for this family so we're always looking for a summer rental. Let me tell you, it's taken a lot of trial and error to come up with the right kind of house for our crew.

"Oh, when I think about some of our rentals! The first time, we thought it would be perfect to find just an ordinary house in the suburbs and put our South American children into a neighbor-hood with other children and invite cousins for the weekends. But it turned out we'd rented in a neighborhood where all the youngsters were in day camp so there was no one to play with until weekends, when the cousins came. And then it seemed that the cousins had no more arrived than it was time for them to leave, so we knew that the next year we'd want a place big enough for cousins to stay longer.

"So the second year we picked another subur-ban house, and we figured we'd do everything just right for the kids. We turned down three great houses at fine prices because we knew we'd have to have a pool before we invited cousins to rotate for a week. Well, it would have worked fine except that there was a water shortage that sum-mer, and we used the pool only two weekends, so two sets of grandchildren felt gypped.

"The third year we swore off pools and went to the shore and rented a big old Victorian house. That was the year it rained the whole month, and we spent the summer with a lot of cranky kids.

"This is our fourth year, and I think maybe we've finally got the hang of our rental needs. We're in a really neat neighborhood. There's a playground at the end of the street, a Y close by with an indoor swimming pool, a shopping mall nearby for the older children, a video rental store five minutes away, a public library with a children's reading hour."

"Sounds perfect," I admitted, "but knowing how children are, I'm sure you'll still have days when they're ornery, and the noise will really get you down. So no matter how you do it, there's still no perfect rental."

"Wrong," she answered quickly. "This time we have the perfect rental. I didn't tell you the whole story. We rented a terrific house with six bedrooms and four baths, and then we rented a one-bedroom house next door. The house next door," she smiled, "is for Herb and me."

I REMEMBER GRANDMA

Once, when I was four years old my grandmother took me downtown (that was back in the days when downtown was a place for grandmothers), and we visited a radio station to see a live talent program. My grandmother obviously thought I was destined to be another Shirley Temple, because family legend has it that when my mother tuned to the station that morning, she heard off-key me singing "I Fall Down and Go Boom."

To commemorate the occasion, Grandma then posed with me for a photographer; that picture is on the back of this book. The other jacket photo is four-year-old Molly with *her* grandmother, me.

And those two pictures are what I think grandparenting is all about.

I think grandparenting is about the ways we learn so that we can perfect the ways we teach.

The link of grandparent to grandchild symbolizes the basic hope for a stable society, a caring family that will guide the growth from generation to generation.

Grandma Wohlgemuth used to take me to the Cleveland Museum of Art, and we'd feed the swans in the reflecting pool outside the museum, and then we'd go inside to see my favorite art (a statue called *Turtle Baby* and Renoir's painting of the girl with a watering can).

If Grandma only knew that when I gave Molly a doll for Christmas Molly promptly named her Mary, in honor of her favorite painter, Mary Cassatt.

My grandmother once took me to a children's matinee to see the film *Alice in Wonderland*, and I was in awe because a story I thought only I knew was so famous that it was actually a movie.

I took my grandson Alex to see *Beauty and the Beast*, and he was so enchanted that a book could be made into a movie that he went to see it time and again with any parent or grandparent who would take him.

I used to bake icebox cookies with my grandmother.

Now Stephanie bakes with her great-grandmother.

Is it any wonder that this is such a special time in my life?

Is it not understandable that my friend who has had more experiences than she can remember and more adventures than she can tell still sits quietly and says, "What I miss in life is grandchildren."

It is for grandchildren that we amass the history, go through the wilds, and take the chances. It is for the grandchildren that we fight the flames and battle the bad guys—not so that we might leave trust funds, but rather that we might leave a legacy of trust.

A child who has a grandparent has a softened view of life, the feeling that there is more to life than what we see, more than getting and gaining, winning and losing.

There is a love that makes no demands.

We share so much with our grandchildren. For both grandparent and grandchild, the parent is the sometime enemy—both of us have protested the actions of those parents without giving up our love for them. Yet we share the knowledge with our grandchildren that we would not have one another if it were not for those parents.

Most of us are not the rule makers with our grandchildren; we have the fun of being rule breakers with them.

We get the joys of parenting without the midnight sniffles and the daytime coughs, without the need for discipline and the demand for obedience.

We are the recess, the play period, the respite from the demands made as they learn to live in a confusing world—and so our grandchildren look to us for good times and laughter.

Is it any wonder that we think grandchildren are so much fun?

THE TEN COMMANDMENTS
OF GRANDPARENTING

Mothers and fathers get courses, textbooks, funny books, serious books, videotapes, books on tape, advice from their peers and from their parents.

But who is there is to advise a grandparent?

Who tells us when to stop nagging and start bragging?

Who tells us when it's time to cut the baby talk and use the big words?

In other words, who is the Dr. Spock of grandparenting?

Obviously we are all out there willy-nilly advising one another whenever it seems to make sense.

But since there isn't always a grandparent on the horizon to advise, here (with apologies to Moses) is an unabridged Ten Commandments for Contemporary Grandparents:

1. Thou shalt not freak out when thy grandchild, to whom thou has just given a one-half interest in Mt. Rushmore plus two Oreo cookies,

refuses to speak to thee on the telephone.
2. Thou shalt permit thy grandchildren to have other grandparents before thee on certain holidays.
3. Thou shalt honor the father and mother of thy grandchildren and thou shalt not substitute thy judgment for theirs.
4. Thou shalt open the doors of thy home and thy heart to thy grandchildren without screaming, "Don't touch," for thou knowest that the visit of thy grandchildren shall soon end.
5. Thou shalt remember thy family history and teach it diligently unto thy grandchildren.
6. Thou shalt refrain from exalting the roles of thy grandchildren, remembering always that thy friends also have grandchildren.
7. Thou shalt not commit effrontery; thou shalt answer the questions of thy grandchildren with dignity and respect.
8. Thou shalt not steal thy grandchild's witticism and pass it as thine own.
9. Thou shalt not covet thy neighbor's grandchild for his or her good grades, sweet disposition, or gentle manner.

10. Thou shalt love thy half-grandchildren, thy stepgrandchildren, thy somewhat grandchildren as surely as thou lovest thy natural grandchildren, for it is the heart not the bloodline that truly makes thee a grandparent.

Grandfathers
are
to
love

THE ABSOLUTE TRUTH
ABOUT GRANDFATHERS

Two businessmen met at their club.

GRANDFATHER #1: Have I shown you the latest pictures of my grandson?

GRANDFATHER #2: No, you haven't, and I've been meaning to thank you.

A father never knew it could be so difficult to raise a child.

A grandfather never knew it could be so easy.

He's a crusty eighty-something New England grandfather who went to Florida for a two-week vacation and came home after four days.

"Dad," his son asked, "are you sick?"

"Nope."

"Homesick?"

"No way."

"Then why did you come home early?"

"Because," Grandpa sniffed, "there are too many old people there."

INTRODUCTION

Once, long before I ever dreamed of being a grandparent, I met a grandfather who told me a charming story about watching television with his granddaughter Cathy. In those days Art Linkletter had an afternoon program on which he talked to children.

One day during the program Mr. Linkletter asked a small boy what grandfathers were for. The child said that grandfathers were for doing nice things, taking you to the circus and out for rides.

Cathy, who was watching the program that day with her grandfather, turned and said, "That's not what I think. I think grandfathers are to love."

When Cathy's grandfather told me the story, I replied blithely that I thought that was a good book title. The grandfather laughed and said that if I'd write it, he'd publish it.

As life turned out, I did and he did.

I wrote the book, and he published it, for the grandfather was George Hecht, and he owned Parents' Magazine Press.

It is many years since the book has been in print. Cathy, that loving granddaughter, is probably herself a loving mother by now.

What brought all this to mind is that after having written so much about grandmothers, it seemed to me only right to give grandfathers some voice in the game, too.

So, in memory of George Hecht and in memory of other grandfathers I have loved with all my heart—here is an updated version of an old love story.

GRANDFATHERS ARE TO LOVE

Sometime between the time tonight
When you put away your blocks,
And the time tomorrow
When you put on your sox . . .
Someone will be thinking of you.

Oh, probably a lot of someones
Will be thinking about you.
Your mommy and your daddy, of course,

And your aunt in Upsaloosa.
The mailman, the sandman,
And the Tooth Fairy
Will all think of you very
Often.

Still this is a different someone.

This is someone
Who thinks of you
Even when you don't
Think of him.

This is a grandfather.

Grandfathers come in all sizes.
They come tall and short,
Hairy and bald,
Thin and fat.
But more than that—

They come when you call them.

That's what grandfathers are for.

For instance, if you need
A dinosaur gaboo
Grandfather would rush right out
To get it just for you.

And should you feel unhappy
And very, very sad.
Who'd cuddle you close?
Why, your darling granddad.

Have a problem with your pup
Or a small alligator?
Where do you get advice?
From your dear old grandpater.

If you have someone to visit
Far far away—
Like two streets from here—
Gramps would take you to play.

And if you played really hard
And came home muddy and sloppy,
Who'd keep parents from scolding?
Your terrific grandpoppy.

Supposing you heard from
Your mother and father

That when they were small,
They really were rather
Exceptional.

Supposing they told you they
Always picked up their clothes,
And that by age one
They could count all ten toes.

Supposing they told you
They were goodies, not baddies.
Who'd tell the truth about them?
Just ask your granddaddies.

And what is the truth about grandfathers?

Just this.
Grandfathers will do
Practically anything
For grandchildren.

They will
Read, feed, and velocipede them.
They will
Play, stay, and holiday them.

They will pinch their cheeks when they're there,
Show their pictures when they're not
And think of them daily.

That's just how grandfathers are.

Dear and sweet and kind,
With just one someone always in mind:
You.

So put your hand in Grandfather's,
Give him your heart, too,
For if you have a grandpa,
Aren't you a lucky you?

Your big hugs and little kisses are what
Grandfathers are made of,
Plus trust and gentle kindness, for
Grandfathers are to love.